Poké Bowl: The best recipes for the H

General information about Poké Bow

Poké Bowl

The best recipes for the new Hawaiian food trend.

Sophia Koch

Poké Bowl: The best recipes for the Hawaiian national dish

What comes to mind first when you think of Hawaii? Probably long, white sandy beaches with palm trees and coconuts. Huge waves conquered by surfers from all over the world, friendly islanders and beautiful women and men.

But do you know the Hawaiian cuisine? A dish which is typical for the country? Honestly, until recently I didn't know any typical Hawaiian dishes myself. Until the day I heard about the Poké Bowls. A dish that slowly but surely is conquering the world.

This is not happening without reason: Poke Bowls are healthy, tasty and quickly prepared!

Poké means "to cut into pieces". To explain it simply, a Poké Bowl is a fish salad that can be made with many different ingredients. This Hawaiian national dish is based primarily on raw fish and rice.

In terms of taste, the Poké Bowl combines Japanese cuisine, such as sushi, with the American West Coast cuisine.

I was invited on vacation and was lucky enough to taste the Poké Bowls. After eating a Poké Bowl for the first time, I couldn't get enough of them.

I prepared a large number of different variations, tried them and invited my friends to dinner. They were all excited and wanted to know how to make them. That led me to the decision to write a recipe book about this great dish myself.

The result is now here before you, in this book I have collected the best recipes that I found.

You will find recipes I got from local Hawaiians, but also recipes that are my own creations, which are now among my friends and family's' favourite dishes.

I hope you enjoy making your own Poké Bowl. Be creative and vary the ingredients. It's a lot of fun and just tastes wonderful.

General information about Poké Bowls

Since the Poké Bowls are made exclusively from fresh vegetables, fruit and fish, you not only have a very tasty meal with the Poké Bowls, but also a very healthy one! It offers lots of vitamins, minerals and also lots of proteins through the fish, which makes this dish perfect even if you do a lot of sports.

With this Hawaiian national dish you have a perfect alternative to the traditional "quickly prepared" dishes, such as burgers, pizza or casseroles. The Poké Bowl is filling but not too heavy on the stomach, which makes it perfect for the summer.
Of course you can prepare and enjoy this dish at any time of the year.

It always tastes good.

Because you don't have to cook or fry anything (except the rice) with the Poké Bowl, the preparation is usually relatively quick and takes no longer than 30 to 60 minutes. Once you have acquired a taste for it and want to prepare a Poké Bowl regularly, I recommend that you precook the rice for several days. Rice keeps relatively long in the fridge and the supply saves you a lot of time during preparation. All other ingredients like the vegetables or especially the fish you should always prepare fresh. And of course it tastes much better fresh!

Poké Bowl with salmon, avocado and spring onion

Cooking time: 30-60min

Ingredients

Servings: 4

- 200 g rice (sushi or round grain, cooked)
- 400 g salmon fillet (sushi quality!)
- 2 avocados (peeled, seeded, diced)
- 100 g spring onion (cut into fine rings)
- 50 g seaweed (dried, e.g. Wakame)
- 4 tbsp Gari (pickled ginger)
- Sesame (black and white, for sprinkling)

For the marinade

- 2 tbsp soy sauce
- 1/2 teaspoon ginger (grated)
- 1 tsp sesame oil (roasted)
- 2 teaspoons lime juice (alternatively lemon juice)

Preparation

First of all for the Poké Bowl with salmon, avocado and spring onions, start by drying the salmon fillet. It's best to dab it off briefly. Then cut the salmon fillet into thick cubes (approx. 1 x 1 cm) and place in the refrigerator for later.

For the marinade, stir all the ingredients thoroughly and mix with the salmon cubes. Leave to marinate in the fridge for about 10 minutes.

Leave the seaweed to soak.

Pour the rice into a bowl, spread the salmon, avocado cubes, seaweed and a tablespoon each of the Gari on the rice. Sprinkle on the spring onion, drizzle on some of the cooled marinade and garnish with sesame seeds. Now you can serve the Poké Bowl with salmon, avocado and spring onions.

Extra tip

You don't like raw fish? No problem! Try the salmon, avocado and spring onion Poké Bowl with tofu instead! Alternatively, you can also fry the salmon cubes in a wok for a short time. This also tastes delicious.

Poké Bowl with tuna, mango and wasabi yoghurt

Cooking time 30-60min

Ingredients

Servings: 4

- 400-450 g tuna (sushi quality!)
- 1 avocado (peeled, seeded, sliced)
- 1 mango (peeled, seeded, diced)
- 200 g quinoa (cooked)
- olive oil
- Gari (pickled ginger)
- Cress (or sprouts, for sprinkling)

For the marinade

- 2 tbsp soy sauce
- 1/2 tbsp soy sauce (sweet)
- 1 tsp sesame oil (roasted)
- 1/2 teaspoon ginger (grated)
- 1/2 tsp garlic (grated)
- 50 g spring onion (cut into rings)
- 50 g shallots (peeled and finely chopped)
- 2 tbsp Wakame (dried seaweed)
- sea salt
- Sesame seeds (black)

For the wasabi yoghurt

- 200 g yoghurt (Greek)
- 1-2 EL Wasabi Powder
- 1 clove of garlic (grated)
- 1/2 lime (juice and zest)
- sea salt

Preparation

For the Poké Bowl with tuna, mango and wasabi yoghurt, start by drying the tuna fillet. It's best to dab it off briefly. Now cut the tuna fillet into slices, then into strips and then into 1x1 cm thick cubes. Now put everything in the fridge. For the marinade, mix all ingredients well and pour over the tuna cubes. Place everything in the fridge for about 10 minutes. Leave to marinate.

For the wasabi yoghurt you have to mix all ingredients well.

Drizzle some olive oil over the quinoa and season with a pinch of salt.

Pour the quinoa into a bowl and arrange the marinated fish, avocado and mango on top. Garnish with wasabi yoghurt, black sesame, gari and cress or sprouts. The Poké Bowl with tuna, mango and wasabi yoghurt is now ready.

Extra tip

Try the Poké Bowl with tuna, mango and wasabi yoghurt with rice, couscous or bulgur!

Poké Bowl with watermelon, macadamia nut and jalapenos

Cooking time: 30-60min

Ingredients

Servings: 4

- 1 watermelon (small, approx. 1 - 1,2 kg, without seeds)
- 1 stick young onion (small, cut into fine rings)
- 2-3 baby cucumber (cut into pieces)
- 100 g macadamia nuts (coarsely chopped)
- 2 tbsp Gari (pickled ginger)
- 1 Jalapeno chili (diced small)
- 1 avocado (peeled, seeded, diced)
- 1 bunch coriander (small)
- Sprouts (for sprinkling, alternatively cress or micro herbs)

For the dressing

- 1 tbsp soy sauce
- 1 clove of garlic (finely grated)
- 2 teaspoons lime juice
- 2 tsp rice wine vinegar
- 1 tablespoon honey (or maple syrup)
- 1/2 tsp sesame oil (roasted)

Preparation

For the Poké Bowl with watermelon, macadamia and jalapeño, start by peeling the watermelon and cut it into 1x1 cm thick cubes. If possible, remove all the seeds.

For the dressing, mix all the ingredients well. Drizzle the dressing on the watermelon cubes and leave to marinate in the refrigerator.

Put the remaining ingredients in the bowl, add the watermelon and pour over the dressing. Next sprinkle with fresh coriander leaves and sprouts. Your Poké Bowl with watermelon, macadamia and jalapeño is now finished.

Extra tip

Enjoy the Poké Bowl with watermelon, macadamia nuts and jalapeño as a refreshing snack between meals or as a main course during the summer!

Poké Bowl with salmon, baby spinach and chili mayonnaise

Cooking time: 30-60min

Ingredients

Servings: 4

- 400-450 g salmon fillet (sushi quality!)
- 200 g rice (round grain or sushi, cooked)
- 150 g Edamame (soybeans, cooked)
- 100 g baby spinach (washed)
- rice wine vinegar
- peanut oil
- sea salt

For the marinade

- 50 ml soy sauce
- 1 tsp rice wine vinegar
- 1 teaspoon ginger (finely grated)
- 1 tsp Sriracha (or chili paste)
- 1 tsp sesame oil (roasted)
- 1/2 tsp honey
- 1 stick young onion (small, cut into fine rings)
- Sesame (black)

For the chili mayonnaise

- 150 g Mayonnaise (light)
- 50 g sour cream
- 1/2 tsp Miso paste
- 1 tsp Chili (fresh, chopped)
- Chili flakes (dried, according to taste)

Preparation

For the Poké Bowl with salmon, baby spinach and chili mayonnaise, first dry the salmon. Then cut it into slices, then into strips and finally into 1x1cm thick cubes and put everything in a cool place.

Now mix all the ingredients for the marinade well and pour over the fish. Let it marinate for 10 minutes in a cool place.
Meanwhile mix all ingredients together for the chili mayonnaise.

Pour the rice into a bowl, press lightly and over-drizzle with the marinade. Season baby spinach with a little rice wine vinegar, peanut oil and sea salt.

Now you can arrange the salmon, Edamame and baby spinach on top and serve with the chili mayonnaise, sesame seeds and green onions. Your Poké Bowl is ready.

Extra tip

The "Poké Bowl" is a Hawaiian dish, which is also becoming more and more popular in Germany! This Poké Bowl with salmon, baby spinach and chili mayonnaise contains the four traditional components: Raw fish, rice, vegetables and marinade. The good thing about Poké Bowls is that they are very versatile. They also taste delicious with tofu or quinoa!

Poké Bowl with tuna, red cabbage and seaweed

Cooking time: 30-60min

Ingredients

Servings: 4

- 200 g rice (sushi or round grain, cooked)
- 400 g tuna fillet (sushi quality!)
- 50 g seaweed (dried; e.g. Wakame)
- 1 avocado (peeled, seeded, cut into slices)
- Sesame (black, for sprinkling)
- 2 baby cucumber (or 1 salad cucumber , planed into wide strips)
- 6 radishes (washed, thinly sliced)

For the marinade

- 2 tbsp soy sauce
- 1/2 teaspoon ginger (grated)
- 1 tsp sesame oil (roasted)
- 2 teaspoons lime juice (or lemon juice)

For the red cabbage

- 1/2 head red cabbage
- 1 tablespoon salt
- 1 tbsp sugar

Preparation

For this Poké Bowl with tuna, red cabbage and seaweed , first dab the tuna fillet dry. Cut it into thick cubes (approx. 1 x 1 cm) and keep in the refrigerator.

For the marinade, stir all the ingredients thoroughly, mix with the tuna cubes and leave to marinate in the fridge for about 10 minutes.

Remove the stalk from the head of red cabbage and cut into fine noodles. Sprinkle with salt and sugar, knead vigorously for a few minutes, then leave to stand for 20 minutes.

Soak the seaweed according to the package instructions and leave to swell.

Pour the rice into bowls and serve with the marinated tuna, red cabbage, seaweed , avocado and radishes. Drizzle some of the remaining marinade top, sprinkle with sesame seeds and serve the tuna, red cabbage and seaweed Poke Bowl.

Extra tip

If you want your Poké Bowl with tuna, red cabbage and seaweed to be particularly spicy, add 1/2 tsp. pressed garlic, 50 g spring onion cut into rings and some chilli flakes to the marinade.

Poké Bowl with salmon, pineapple and Chioggia turnip

Cooking time: 30-60min

Ingredients

Servings: 4

- 200 g rice (sushi or round grain, cooked)
- 400 g salmon fillet (sushi quality!)
- 2 baby cucumber (or 1 cucumber, sliced)
- 1/2 pineapple (peeled, diced)
- 1 bell pepper (red, cleaned, cut into slices)
- 50 g seaweed (dried, e.g. Nori and Wakame)
- 400 g Chioggia beet
- Sesame (black and white, for sprinkling)

For the marinade

- 2 tbsp soy sauce
- 1/2 teaspoon ginger (grated)
- 1 tsp sesame oil (roasted)
- 2 teaspoons lime juice (or lemon juice)

Preparation

For the Poké Bowl with salmon, pineapple and Chioggia beet you must first dry the salmon fillet. Cut the salmon fillet into thick cubes (approx. 1x1 cm) and put in the fridge until next step.

For the marinade you have to mix all ingredients thoroughly and add the salmon cubes. Let it marinate in the fridge for about 10 minutes.

Clean the Chioggia beet and cut into 2mm thin slices.

Soak the seaweed according to the package

instructions and leave to swell.

Pour rice into a bowl, arrange with salmon, pineapple cubes, Chioggia beet, paprika, seaweed and cucumber. Drizzle with a little of the remaining marinade and sprinkle with sesame seeds. Now you can serve the Poké Bowl with salmon, pineapple and Chioggia beet.

Extra tip

The red and white Chioggia beet is a subspecies of the red beet and comes originally from the Chioggia peninsula in the Veneto region. It tastes sweeter and not as earthy as the "classic" beetroot. Chioggia beets have an appetising effect and a particularly high iron content. This supports haemoglobin levels.

Poké Bowl with tuna, avocado and lemongrass

Cooking time: 30-60min

Ingredients

Servings: 4

- 200 g rice (sushi, alternatively round grain, cooked)
- 400 g tuna fillet (sushi quality)
- 2 avocados (peeled, seeded, finely diced)
- 2 sticks lemongrass (young sticks absolutely!)
- 2 tbsp sesame seeds (white)
- For the marinade:
- 2 tbsp soy sauce
- 1/2 teaspoon ginger (grated)
- 1 tsp sesame oil (roasted)
- 2 teaspoons lime juice (alternatively lemon juice)

Preparation

For the Tuna Poké Bowl with avocado and lemon grass you first have to prepare the fish: Dab the tuna fillet dry, dice it into small cubes (approx. 1x1cm) and put it in the fridge until further processing.

For the marinade you have to mix all ingredients thoroughly with the fish cubes. Let it marinate in the fridge for about 10 minutes.

Wash lemon grass and chop into short strips.
Mix the avocado pieces with the marinated tuna cubes.

Put the rice in a bowl. Spread the tuna-avocado mixture on top and drizzle with the remaining marinade.
Sprinkle with 1/2 tablespoon sesame seeds and garnish with the lemongrass chunks. The Poké Bowl is ready.

Extra tip

For the Tuna Poké Bowl with avocado and lemongrass, definitely use young lemongrass sticks, because the older the sticks are, the more woody their fibres are! The fine taste of the sticks is also lost with age.

Ahi Poké Bowl with sprouts and fried onion

Cooking time: 30-60min

Ingredients

Servings: 4

- 200 g rice (sushi, alternatively round grain, cooked)
- 400 g salmon fillet (sushi quality)
- 2 avocados (peeled, seeded, finely diced)
- 2 handfuls of rungs (of your choice, e.g. watercress)
- 1 stick of spring onion (small, cut into fine rings)
- 2 tablespoons sesame seeds (black and white mixed)
- 100 g roasted onion

For the marinade

- 2 tbsp soy sauce
- 1/2 teaspoon ginger (grated)
- 1 tsp sesame oil (roasted)
- 2 teaspoons lime juice

Preparation

For the Ahi Poké Bowl with sprouts and roasted onion, first prepare the roasted onion according to the basic recipe.

Dab the salmon fillet dry, cut into cubes and put in the fridge.

For the marinade, mix all the ingredients thoroughly with the salmon cubes. Let it marinate in the fridge for about 10 minutes.

Wash the sprouts and cut them necessary.

Put the rice in a bowl. Spread the marinated salmon, avocado and fried onion over the rice. Sprinkle on some sprouts, spring onion and 1/2 tablespoon sesame seeds and drizzle on the remaining marinade to taste. The Poké Bowl is ready.

Extra tip

The marinade for the Ahi Poké Bowl with sprouts and fried onion is a "basic marinade". You can extend this marinade according to your taste: for example with garlic, chilli, seaweed , rice wine vinegar.

Fiery Poké Bowl with salmon

Cooking time: 30-60min

Ingredients

Servings: 4

- 450 g salmon fillet
- 60 ml soy sauce
- 1 teaspoon rice vinegar
- 1 teaspoon Sriracha or chilli paste
- 1 teaspoon sesame oil
- 300 g rice
- 3 spring onions
- 1 avocado
- 2 Minigurken
- 1 bunch radish
- 200 g Wakame seaweed salad
- 300 g brown rice

For the Sriracha sauce

- 2 tablespoons Sriracha
- 2 tablespoons Greek yoghurt

Cook the rice according to the instructions on the packet.

Dice salmon fillet (approx. 1x1cm). Mix vinegar, sesame oil, soy sauce and Sriracha with the salmon and put in the fridge.

Cut the cucumber and radishes into fine slices. Peel, core and dice the avocado. Cut the green halves of the spring onions into fine rings.

Mix Greek yoghurt and Sriracha for the Sriracha sauce.

Put the boiled rice in a bowl. Add salmon, poké and cucumber and drizzle with Sriracha sauce. The Poké Bowl is ready.

Extra tip

You can also use salad instead of rice as a base for the Poké Bowl.

Poké Bowl with prawns, mango and sesame seeds

Cooking time: 30-60min

Ingredients

Servings 4

- 480 ml rice vinegar
- 12 tablespoons soy sauce
- 8 tablespoons sesame paste (Tahina)
- 8 limes
- 2 teaspoons sugar
- 600 g peeled prawns
- 4 spring onions
- 2 Mango
- 8 tablespoons Wakame Seaweed Salad

- 1 avocado
- 2 small head of lettuce
- pickled ginger
- sesame
- coriander

Preparation

Wash the salad thoroughly and cut into smaller pieces. Let it drip off briefly.

Grate the lime peel and squeeze out the limes. Bring rice vinegar, soy sauce, sesame paste, lime peel, juice and sugar to the boil in a small pot. Stir with a whisk until the sauce thickens and combines slightly. Leave to cool and put in the fridge.

Peel and chop the mango. Cut the spring onions into rings. Remove the avocado pit and remove the flesh from the skin with a spoon. Then dice the avocado.

Stir-fry the prawns in a small pan with oil for about 1 minute on each side and then place in the sauce.

Now put the salad in a bowl as a base. Put mango, avocado, wakame and prawns with sauce on top and arrange with spring onions, pickled ginger, sesame and coriander leaves.

Extra tip As an alternative to frying, you can also cook the prawns in salted water. When the meat turns white/pink/orange, the shrimps are ready.

Poké Bowl with cucumber and creamy salmon

Cooking time: 30-60min

Ingredients

Servings 4

For the Togarashi sauce

- 80 g mayonnaise
- 1/2 teaspoon Mirin
- 3 teaspoons Sriracha
- 1 piece ginger (approx. 1cm)
- 1 1/2 teaspoon soy sauce
- 1/4 teaspoon sugar
- 1/2 teaspoon salt
- 1/4 teaspoon pepper

For the Poké

- 500 g salmon fillet
- 3 spring onions
- 300 g brown rice

For the pickled cucumber

- 2 Mini cucumber
- 120 ml rice vinegar
- 120 ml water
- 80 ml honey
- 1 teaspoon salt
- 1/2 teaspoon chili flakes

Preparation

Cook the brown rice according to the package instructions.

For the Togarashi sauce, mix the mayonnaise and the other ingredients and put in the fridge.

Cut the white half of the spring onions into fine rings.

Dice the salmon and add (approx. 1x1cm). Stir in about 2 tablespoons of the Togarashi sauce.

Heat a pot at the highest heat and add the pickled cucumber , vinegar, water, honey, salt and chilli flakes. When everything is boiling, add the cucumber slices and stir well. Let it cool for 10 minutes, remove the cucumber and put it in the fridge.

Put the rice in a bowl.

Add salmon poké and pickled cucumber . Cut the green halves of the spring onions into fine slices and spread over the poké. The Poké Bowl is ready.

Extra tip

If you like it a bit more exotic you can mix the Togarashi sauce with 2 teaspoons of Togarashi Shichimi, a Japanese spice mixture of ground red chillies, red Japanese pepper, roasted orange peel, black and white sesame seeds, hemp seeds and ground ginger.

Poké Bowl California Roll

Cooking time: 15-30min

Ingredients

Portions 6

- 400g crab meat or Surimi
- 3 pcs. Spring onions
- 120g Japanese cucumber or salad cucumber
- 1 pc. Avocado
- 2 tbsp Masago or Tobiko (fish roes)
- 4 tsp sesame oil
- 2 tbsp soy sauce
- 2 tablespoons roasted sesame seeds
- 1 pinch of sea salt flakes

Ingredients for Sriracha mayonnaise

- ½ cup mayonnaise
- 2 tbsp Sriracha chilli sauce
- 2 tbsp rice vinegar
- 1 pinch salt

Ingredients for garnishing

- 1 packet of Nori seaweed cut into strips
- 1 tsp Japanese cress

Preparation

First mix the mayonnaise, Sriracha sauce and rice vinegar well and season to taste with salt.
Wash and clean the spring onions and cut them into thin rings. Wash the cucumber as well and cut it into thin slices or small cubes as desired. Now peel the avocado and stone it. Then cut into small cubes.

Put the crab meat together with the vegetables in a bowl. Add the masago or tobiko, sesame oil, soy sauce, sesame seeds and half of the Sriracha mayonnaise and mix well. Now sprinkle the whole with sea salt flakes. Now add the Roll Poké. If you still have crab pieces left you can garnish the Poké Bowl with them, Nori seaweed and cress or radish sprouts.

It goes well with rice or simply a crispy piece of bread of your choice.

Extra tip Instead of the avocado you can use mango or banana. This makes the Roll Poké more fruity and gives it a sweet touch.

Poké Bowl with Cauliflower, Sesame and Avocado

Cooking time: 30-60min

Ingredients

Servings 4

- 1 cauliflower
- 2 tbsp sesame seeds
- 3 spring onions
- 4 - 5 mushrooms
- 1 bell pepper
- 1 avocado
- 200 g small tomatoes
- 4 tbsp soy sauce (without sugar)
- 1 tbsp sesame oil
- Chilli flakes to taste
- 200 g salmon fresh or pickled

Preparation

Start by grating the cauliflower. Then fry the cauliflower rice in a coated pan without oil until it has a light browning.

Put the cauliflower rice aside and roast the sesame while the pan is still hot. You should not use oil here either.

Cut the spring onions into small rings and the mushrooms into slices.

Remove the stalk and the seeds from the pepper and cut them into strips. Remove the seed from the avocado and cut the avocado in half.
Now you can simply peel off the skin and cut the avocado into strips or cubes. Finally you halve the small tomatoes.

Stir the marinade together. Take a bowl and mix the soy

sauce with chilli flakes to taste. Then add the sesame oil.

As a last step in the preparation marinate the salmon together with the spring onions in the marinade for 10 minutes.

Put everything in a bowl and garnish the Poké Bowl with salmon, fried cauliflower rice and roasted sesame seeds.

Poké Bowl with tofu, radish and Ponzu dressing

Cooking time: 30-60min

Ingredients

Servings 4

- 400-450 g Tofu (natural or smoked)
- 2 tbsp Nori leaves (cut into fine strips)
- 200 g rice (round grain or brown rice, cooked)
- 2 baby cucumber (peeled in slices with the peeler)
- 6 radishes (sliced)
- Daikon cress (alternatively mizuna or micro herbs)

For the Ponzu dressing

- 2 1/2 tbsp olive oil
- 2 tbsp sesame oil (roasted)
- 2 tbsp Yuzu juice (alternatively a mix of lime and lemon juice)
- 1 tbsp rice wine vinegar
- 1 tbsp Mirin
- 1/2 teaspoon ginger (finely grated)
- 1 tbsp Mirin
- 2 tbsp honey
- 2 tbsp soy sauce
- 2 tbsp Wakame
- 1 stick young onion (small, cut into fine rings)

Preparation

For the Poké Bowl with tofu, radish and Ponzu dressing cut the tofu into slices, then into strips and 1x1 cm thick cubes.

For the marinade you must mix all the ingredients thoroughly and pour over the tofu. Let it marinate in the fridge for about 10 minutes.

Pour the rice into a bowl and drizzle a little of the marinade over it.

Spread the tofu cubes, cucumber and radishes over the rice and sprinkle with the chopped nori leaves and Daikon cress. The Poké Bowl is ready.

Extra tip

The Poké Bowl with tofu, radish and Ponzu dressing can of course be further refined with vegetables of your choice and prepared according to your taste.

Poké Bowl with pineapple and tofu

Cooking time: 30-60min

Ingredients

Servings 4

For the tofu

- 800 g solid tofu
- 120 ml sesame oil
- 120 ml soy sauce
- 4 tablespoons pineapple juice
- 2 tablespoons rice vinegar
- 2 pieces ginger (approx. 1 cm)
- 2 teaspoons sesame seeds
- 1/2 teaspoon chili garlic sauce
- 2 Organic lime

For the Poké

- 400 g pineapple
- 2 avocado
- 2 Lime
- 300 g cucumber
- 2 Carrot
- 140 g quinoa
- 2 chili
- Chives to garnish

Preparation

Wash the quinoa preparation in a sieve with fresh water and cook according to the instructions on the packet.

Peel and grate or finely chop the ginger (the smaller the better). Grate the lime peel and squeeze out the juice. Mix the ginger, lime peel and juice with the remaining ingredients of the marinade.

Dice the tofu (approx. 1x1cm) and add. Allow to stand for at least 5 minutes.

Now peel the pineapple, quarter it and remove the fibrous core. Chop the flesh. Peel the avocado and remove the seeds. Cut avocado and cucumber into fine slices and sprinkle with lime juice. Peel the carrot and chop or grate it finely. Cut the chilli and chives into small strips or rolls.

Put the quinoa in a bowl and cover with tofu, pineapple, cucumber and carrot. Garnish with the rest of the marinade. Sprinkle with chives, chilli and sesame seeds. The Poké Bowl is ready.

Extra tip

You can also mix the chilli garlic sauce yourself. Add a small clove of garlic and mix with ½ Teaspoon Sriracha. If you don't like it that hot, you can cut the fresh chilli in half and remove the seeds and skins.

Vegan Poké Bowl with Peanut Tofu

Cooking time: 30-60min

Ingredients

Servings 2

- 200 g Tofu Nature
- 2 tbsp peanut butter (not to be confused with peanut butter)
- 1 tbsp sesame oil
- 1 tbsp soy sauce
- 2 tbsp. lemon or lime juice or half a lemon/one lime
- Chili flakes as desired
- 1 tbsp sesame seeds
- 1 cucumber
- 80 g red cabbage or pink pointed cabbage
- 100 g frozen dam (from Bio-TK) or peas

- 3-4 radishes per serving (depending on size and preference)
- 4 spring onions
- 1 avocado
- Fresh coriander to taste

Optional: chili threads and black/light sesame seeds for garnishing

For the sushi rice

- 200 g Sushi rice
- 2 tbsp rice vinegar
- 1 tbsp Mirin
- 1 tbsp sake (optional)
- 2 teaspoons rice syrup or apple syrup
- sea salt
- 4 tbsp lemon juice or a juicy lemon

Preparation

Preheat oven to 200°C circulating air.

Remove 200 g tofu from the packaging and press dry with several layers of kitchen paper and cut the tofu into small cubes.

Mix 2 tbsp. peanut butter, 1 tbsp. sesame oil, 1 tbsp. soy sauce, 2 tbsp. lemon or lime juice, 1-2 tsp. rice syrup and chilli flakes well and spread the tofu pieces over it.

Now place the marinated tofu pieces in an ovenproof dish.

Marinate the tofu with peanut sauce. The longer you leave everything in the fridge, the stronger the taste becomes.

Bake the tofu in the oven at 200°C circulating air for about 30 minutes.

Mix everything briefly every so often.

Now mix 1 tablespoon roasted sesame seeds with the baked tofu.

Use a julienne slicer to plane medium sized strips from the cucumber . Now season the cucumber spirals with a little lemon juice and salt. Cut 80 g red cabbage into fine slices. Defrost 100 g Edamame in warm water. Wash the radishes and cut them into thin slices. Wash the spring onions and cut them into small rolls.

Bring the rice to the boil with about 220 ml of water. If necessary, add some water during cooking and cook for a total of 8-10 minutes. Remove the pan from the heat and let the rice soak for 10 minutes with the lid on.

Mix 2 tbsp rice vinegar, 1 tbsp mirin, 1 small tbsp sake (optional), 2 tsp rice syrup or apple syrup, sea salt and 1 tbsp lemon juice and mix with the rice.

Divide the rice into two bowls and then spread the Edamame, the grated red cabbage and the cucumber nest on top. Pour the warm, baked tofu into the centre of the Poké Bowl. Finish the Poké Bowl with the radish slices and avocado pieces.

Garnish the Poké Bowl with the sliced spring onions, sesame seeds, chilli flakes and chilli threads. The Poké Bowl is ready.

Extra tip

You can drizzle lemon juice on th Poké Bowl to taste, season with soy sauce or finish with hot Sriracha chili sauce.

Vegan Poké Bowl with Chick Peas, Grilled Vegetables and Avocado

Cooking time: 30-60min

Ingredients

Servings 4

For the Spicy Crunchy Chickpeas

- 800 g chickpeas in a tin (drained net weight)
- 4 tbsp olive oil
- 2 teaspoons salt
- 2 tsp black pepper, freshly ground
- 2 tsp cayenne pepper, ground
- 2 tsp onion powder, granulated
- 2 teaspoons garlic powder
- 2 tsp turmeric
- 2 handfuls parsley, freshly chopped

For the Wasabi-Mayo alternative

- 200 g vegan mayonnaise substitute
- 200 g soy yoghurt alternative, natural
- 1 pc. Avocado
- 6 TL Wasabi paste
- 1 piece orange, juice freshly pressed Orange, juice freshly squeezed
- 4 tsp vegan soy sauce
- 2 TL ORGANIC AGAVE NECTAR
- 200 g natural wild rice mixture
- 300 g tofu prawns (giant prawns from Lord of Tofu)
- some olive oil, for frying & baking
- 1 pc. Avocado
- 8 pcs. mini peppers Mini peppers
- 8 slices pineapple
- 2 teaspoons sugar
- some leaf salad (e.g. Fresée salad)

- 2 handfuls Hot Wasabi-Mix (peas and peanuts snack with wasabi flavour)

Preparation

Put the chickpeas in a strainer, drain the liquid and wash them thoroughly with fresh water. When the chickpeas are dry, put them in a bowl. Add 2 tablespoons of olive oil and toss thoroughly.

Spread the chick peas on a baking tray lined with baking paper and bake in a preheated oven at 220°C for 25 minutes. After about half the baking time, briefly mix the chickpeas once.
Mix all the spices (preferably in a small bowl) and put them in the oven with the chickpeas.

Wash the mini peppers thoroughly and pat dry. Place the pineapple slices and peppers on a baking tray lined with baking paper and brush with a little olive oil. Refine the pineapple slices with a little sugar. Grill the paprika and pineapple in the oven. The remaining heat from the previous baking of the chickpeas should be enough. As soon as they have some colour they are ready.

Put all the ingredients for the vegetable cream in a kitchen blender and mix to a creamy salad mayonnaise. Add some salt and pepper to taste.

Cook the rice according to the package instructions and place in a bowl. Lightly fry the giant tofu prawns in a little olive oil. Cut the avocado into fine slices or cubes. Now arrange the whole thing in the bowl and garnish with the wasabi mix and fresh herbs. The Poké Bowl is ready.

Vegan Poké Bowl with sesame, almond and smoked tofu

Cooking time: 30-60min

Ingredients

Servings 2

- 130 g round grain natural rice
- 1 small sweet potato, peeled and diced (approx. 200 g)
- 1/2 tablespoon or more of olive oil
- Sea salt and freshly ground black pepper
- 100 g broccolini (Bimi) or broccoli florets
- 4 stems of green asparagus, cut into pieces
- 4 radishes, thinly sliced
- 1 mini cucumber , thinly sliced
- 1 medium carrot, grated
- 1 spring onion, thinly sliced

- 100 g Sesame-almond smoked tofu, thinly sliced

For the dressing

- 1 1/2 tbsp soy sauce
- 1 teaspoon roasted sesame oil
- 1/2 tablespoon rice vinegar, unseasoned (Japanese)
- 1 teaspoon freshly grated ginger
- 1 small clove of garlic, crushed

Preparation Boil the rice for about 30-40 minutes in double the amount of water until the rice grains are soft and the water is absorbed. Let the rice cool down and put it aside for now.

Heat the oven to 200°C and lay out a baking tray with baking paper.

Spread the sweet potato pieces on the prepared baking tray and add some olive oil.

Now distribute the sweet potato pieces evenly on the baking tray. Make sure that the pieces are not on top of each other, otherwise they will not bake evenly. Then season with salt and pepper according to taste and place the tray in the oven at medium height. The sweet potato pieces should roast in the oven until they are soft and crispy at the edges (approx. 25-30 minutes).

In between you should turn the sweet potato pieces once.

Blanch the broccolini and asparagus in a large pot of boiling salted water until the vegetables are al dente. This takes about 3 minutes. Let the vegetables drip off in a sieve and scare them off briefly with ice-cold water. Sieve everything again and then dry the vegetables with a dry towel.

In a small bowl, mix the soy sauce, sesame oil, rice vinegar, ginger and garlic.

Arrange the Poké Bowl with a generous spoonful of rice, broccolini, asparagus, radish, cucumber , carrot, spring onion, tofu and the sweet potato and spread the dressing over it. Garnish the Poké Bowl with some fresh coriander and sesame seeds. The Poké Bowl is ready.

Extra tip

Precooking rice! Then it's a bit easier to prepare the vegan Poké Bowl if you want it to go fast.

Closing words

Of course, the Poké Bowl recipes listed here are just a few of the many I have tried. I like them very much and I can only recommend that you prepare and taste each recipe individually!

But the Poké Bowls also offer a lot of scope for your own creations. Just use your favourite ingredients for your own individual Poké Bowl and let your creativity run wild. There are virtually no limits to the Poké Bowl.

Made in United States
Troutdale, OR
01/11/2024